ABC Zoo

Written by Jean Warren

Illustrated by Judy Shimono

Warren Publishing House, Inc.
Everett, Washington

Special thanks to Jeannie Lybecker, children's literature specialist, for compiling the list of books about the zoo found on page 24. For information about these books or other children's literature, write Ms. Lybecker at Early Childhood Bookhouse, P.O. Box 2791, Portland, OR 97208.

Some of the activity ideas in this book were originally contributed by *Totline Newsletter* subscribers. We wish to acknowledge: Sue Brown, Louisville, KY; Cindy Dingwall, Palatine, IL; Barbara B. Fleisher, Glen Oaks, NY; Judy Hall, Wytheville, VA; Joelene Holley-Thomas, Kennewick, WA; Sharon Olson, Minot, ND; Susan M. Paprocki, Northbrook, IL; Paula Schneider, Kent, WA; Betty Silkunas, Lansdale, PA; Becky Valenick, Rockford, IL.

Editor: Gayle Bittinger
Editorial Assistants: Kathleen Cubley, Susan M. Sexton
Production Manager: Eileen Carbary
Design: Kathy Kotomaimoce
Computer Graphics: Eric Stovall
Production Assistant: Jo Anna Brock
Cover Illustration: Larry Countryman

ISBN 0-911019-41-3

Library of Congress Catalog Card Number: 90-071743
Printed in the United States of America
Published by: Warren Publishing House, Inc.
            P.O. Box 2250
            Everett, WA 98203

20 19 18 17 16 15 14 13 12 11 10 9 8 7 6 5 4 3 2

Animals in the Jungle

Set out a box of scraps of fake fur. Let each child choose one or two of the scraps to glue onto a piece of posterboard. Using the scraps as animal bodies, have the children add heads, legs and tails with felt-tip markers. Let the children glue on pieces of grass to finish their jungle scenes.

Zoo Sticker Collages

Give each child a piece of green construction paper. Set out an assortment of animal stickers. Let each child choose five or six stickers to put on his or her paper. Let the children glue grass, small leaves or twigs to their papers to create zoo collages.

Yarn Snakes

Give the children large pieces of construction paper and lengths of thick yarn. Have the children lay their yarn pieces in pans of brown tempera paint. Then let them wiggle and slither their paint-covered yarn across their papers. When they are done have them coil their yarn around and around on their papers and let them dry.

Paper Snakes

Let the children color paper plates with tempera paint, crayons or felt-tip markers. Turn each plate into a "snake" by cutting it as shown. Hang the paper snakes from the ceiling.

Variation: Instead of paper plates, cut circles out of green construction paper. Have the children dab brown tempera paint on the circles to represent snake skin. Then cut the circles as shown.

Paper Bag Elephants

For each child cut a paper bag so that it lays flat. Let the children crinkle their bags by grabbing them in different spots and squeezing them. Then have them flatten out their bags and paint them with gray tempera paint. When the paint has dried, cut a large elephant shape out of each child's bag. Have the children glue on button or construction paper eyes and use felt-tip markers to add mouths.

Jungle Animal Masks

Let the children use paper plates to create animal masks. Cut eye holes out of the plates and cut nose and ear shapes out of construction paper. Let each child choose to make one of the following masks:

Zebra — Paint black vertical stripes on the back side of a plate. When the paint has dried, glue on nose and ear shapes. Then glue pieces of crepe paper streamers around the edge of the plate. (To keep paint from smearing, glue ears and streamers on the unpainted side of the mask.)

Leopard — Paint the back side of a paper plate yellow. When the paint has dried, use a black felt-tip marker or black paint to make spots. Add nose and ear shapes and crepe paper streamers.

Elephant — Paint the back side of a paper plate gray. Glue on trunk, ears and streamers.

When the children have finished, display their masks as room decorations or attach tongue depressors for handles and let the children use their masks for dramatic play.

Fuzzy Bears

For each child cut a bear shape out of brown construction paper or a brown paper bag. Have the children brush glue all over their bear shapes. Then let the children sprinkle sawdust or rinsed coffee grounds over the glue to make "fuzzy" brown bears.

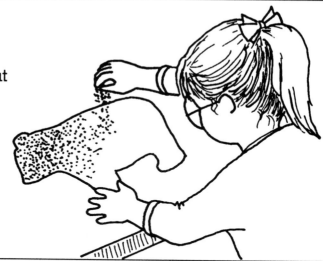

Cotton Ball Panda Bears

Cut small bear shapes out of black construction paper. Use a hole punch to punch out small black circles for eyes. Cut green construction paper into thin triangles for bamboo leaves. Have the children glue the bear shapes on pieces of light blue construction paper. Then have them each glue one cotton ball on the bear's face and another cotton ball (slightly stretched out) on the body, leaving a little of the black construction paper showing between the two. Show them how to glue the black circles on their bears' faces for eyes. Then let them each glue on a row of toothpicks or wooden skewers to make bamboo stalks before adding the leaf shapes.

What Is a Zoo?

Tell the children about zoos. Explain to them that a zoo is a place where people can safely see wild animals. The animals live in areas that resemble, as much as possible, the environment they came from. It takes many people to care for the animals at the zoo. Have the children help name the jobs that need to be done at the zoo such as feeding the animals, taking care of the animals health, keeping the grounds clean and giving tours of the zoo.

Animal Families

Set out a collection of wild animal pictures. Let the children take turns sorting the animals into "families." For example tigers, panthers and lions are in the cat family, monkeys, gorillas and chimpanzees are in the ape family, black bears, brown bears, polar bears and panda bears are in the bear family; flamingos, parrots and toucans are in the bird family and snakes, lizards, alligators and iguanas are in the reptile family.

Learning About Wild Animals

Each day pick a different wild animal to learn about. Using a large tray, a box or a sand table, create the environment the animal lives in such as a forest, a jungle, the plains or a swamp. Using books, help the children discover facts about the animal such as what it likes to eat, what the animal looks like, what kinds of sounds the animal makes and where it sleeps.

Sorting Zoo Animals

Set out a collection of plastic zoo animals. Let the children sort them by size. Have them name the animals. Or let the children sort the animals into the following three groups: animals that walk on land, animals that swim in the water and animals that fly in the air.

Graham Cracker Animals

In a blender combine ¼ cup unsweetened frozen apple juice concentrate, ¼ cup vegetable oil, 1 sliced banana, 1 teaspoon vanilla and 1 teaspoon cinnamon. In a large bowl, mix together 1 cup graham flour, 1 cup whole-wheat flour, ½ teaspoon baking soda and ½ teaspoon salt. Add the apple juice mixture to the flour mixture and stir thoroughly. Roll out the dough on a floured surface and cut out animal shapes with a cookie cutter. Bake at 350 degrees for 8 minutes. Serve the animal crackers plain or let the children spread them with peanut butter. Makes 2 to 3 dozen animals. Encourage the children to name each animal shape before eating it.

Zoo Snacks

Each day have the children pretend to be a different kind of zoo animal at snacktime and feed them a snack that those animals would eat. For example, on Elephant Day serve the children peanuts, bread and vegetables; on Monkey Day, serve them bananas and on Bear Day serve them berries, apples and vegetables.

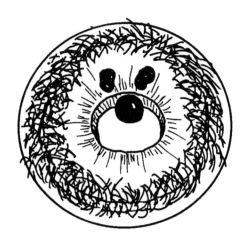

Lion Salad

Place pineapple rings on small plates to use as lion heads. Let the children add shredded carrots for manes, cherries for noses and raisins for eyes.

Banana Snacks

Banana Pops — Stick Popsicle sticks into banana halves. Dip the bananas into a mixture of equal parts of lemon juice and water. Roll the bananas in nut-like cereal. Place on waxed paper and freeze.

Nutty Bananas — Make a mixture of finely grated nuts, wheat germ and cinnamon. Give each child a small amount of the mixture on a plate plus a banana half with the peel still on. Have the children gradually peel their bananas and dip them into their nut mixture before each bite.

Banana Milkshake — Blend 1 cup milk and 1 sliced banana together for a delicious milkshake. Makes three 4-ounce servings.

Banana Sandwich — Split a banana lengthwise. Spread one side of the banana with peanut butter. Put the banana halves back together. Slice the banana into bite-sized pieces.

Vegetable Animals

Cut a variety of vegetables such as carrots, celery, zucchini, radishes, potatoes and turnips into wedges, circles and sticks. Give the children the vegetable shapes and toothpicks. Encourage the children to make wild vegetable animals by sticking various vegetable pieces together. Let the children eat their wild animals as is or provide a Ranch dressing dip. (*Note:* Be sure the children remove the toothpicks before eating their creations.)

Cheese Animal Sandwiches

Set out slices of cheese and various animal cookie cutters. Let each child choose a cookie cutter and help him or her cut out the shape in a piece of cheese. Place the cheese animal shape on a slice of bread. Let the children eat their cheese animal sandwiches as is or slightly toasted in the oven.

Monkeys See, Monkeys Do

Have the children stand in a circle and pretend to be monkeys. Choose one child to make a movement and have the other children try to imitate it. Continue until all the children have been chosen to lead a movement.

Variation: Repeat the following rhyme as the children play this game. Change the second line each time to indicate the actions chosen by the child in the middle of the circle.

Monkeys, monkeys in the tree.
Can you jump around like me?
Monkeys see, monkeys do,
Little monkeys in the zoo.

Jean Warren

Zoo Hokey-Pokey

Have the children sing and move like their favorite zoo animals while doing the Hokey-Pokey. Let the children take turns picking out an animal to imitate and the part of the animal's body to sing about. For example, "You shake your mane in; You stick your giraffe neck in; You wiggle your snake belly in; You jump your kangaroo legs in."

Zoo Train

Have the children line up in a row to make a zoo train. Designate one area in the room to be the train station. Let the first child in line be the Engineer. Have the children sing the first verse of this song with you:

Sung to: "Down by the Station"

Down by the station,
Next to the zoo,
On came an animal,
Do you know who?

Let the Engineer tell what animal came aboard the train and what action that animal is performing. For example, he or she might say "A kangaroo came aboard and it is hopping." Then let the children sing the rest of the song with you as the train "hops" around the room:

We picked up a kangaroo,
And what do you know,
This is the way
The train started to go.
Hopping, hopping, watch us go,
Hopping fast, then hopping slow.
Hopping down, hopping back.
All around the track.

Jean Warren

When the train returns to the station, have the Engineer go to the back of the line. Then let the child at the front of the line become the new Engineer and choose the next animal. Continue playing until everyone has had a turn being the Engineer.

Did You Ever See the Animals?

Sing or chant the following movement rhyme. Have the children act out each animal's movement.

Sung to: "Did You Ever See a Lassie?"

Did you ever see a monkey,
A monkey, a monkey?
Did you ever see a monkey swing
This way and that?
Swing this way and that way
And this way and that way?
Did you ever see a monkey swing
This way and that?

Additional verses: "Did you ever see a kangaroo jump this way and that? Did you ever see a lion roar this way and that? Did you ever see an elephant walk this way and that? Did you ever see a snake crawl this way and that?"

Judy Hall

If I Were

Have the children act out the motions while you recite the poem below. If desired, continue with verses of your own.

If I were a tiny snake,
I'd slither all around.
If I were a tiny snake,
I'd crawl across the ground.

If I were an elephant,
I'd swing my trunk around.
If I were an elephant,
I'd stomp across the ground.

If I were a kangaroo,
I'd jump and jump around.
If I were a kangaroo,
I'd jump across the ground.

Paula Schneider

Elephant Walk

Read the poem below out loud and have the children act out the motions.

Right foot, left foot, see me go.
> (Put weight on one foot then the other, swaying from side to side.)

I am gray and big and slow.
> (Walk slowly around the room.)

I come walking down the street

With my trunk and four big feet.
> (Extend arms together in front and swing them like a trunk.)

Author Unknown

Can You Guess?

Have the children sit in a circle. Choose one child at a time to go into the middle of the circle and imitate a zoo animal. Let the children try to guess what animal it is. If no one can guess, ask the child to make the animal's sound. If a child has trouble thinking of an animal, whisper the name of an animal in his or her ear. Continue the game until each child has had a chance to be in the middle of the circle.

Polar Bear, Polar Bear

Let the children act out the following rhyme.

Polar bear, polar bear walk around.
Polar bear, polar bear lay on the ground.
Polar bear, polar bear jump in the sea.
Polar bear, polar bear swim to me.

Jean Warren

The Zoo

Sung to: "The Mulberry Bush"

Get in the car and we'll go to the zoo,
Go to the zoo, go to the zoo.
Get in the car and we'll go to the zoo,
Early in the mornin'.

We will see lions and tigers and bears,
Tigers and bears, tigers and bears.
We will see lions and tigers and bears,
Early in the mornin'.

We will see fish and spiders and snakes,
Spiders and snakes, spiders and snakes.
We will see fish and spiders and snakes,
Early in the mornin'.

All kinds of animals live at the zoo,
Live at the zoo, live at the zoo.
All kinds of animals live at the zoo,
Early in the mornin'.

Becky Valenick

At the Zoo

Sung to: "If You're Happy and You Know It"

Did you ever watch the animals at the zoo?
It's such fun to watch the animals at the zoo.
There are birds of red and blue,
Polar bears and monkeys too.
It's such fun to watch the animals at the zoo.

Sue Brown

Look What I See
Sung to: "Up on the Housetop"

Down at the zoo we will find,
Animals of most every kind.
Elephants, bears and kangaroos,
Birds and snakes will be there too!
Oh, oh, oh, look what I see,
Oh, oh, oh, look what I see.
Down at the zoo we will find
Animals of most every kind.

Cindy Dingwall

Going to the Zoo
Sung to: "Yankee Doodle"

If you're going to the zoo,
Remember who will meet you.
Tigers, zebras, porcupines,
And monkeys they will greet you.
Next you'll see the king of all,
And lion is his name.
The giraffes and elephants
Will all be glad you came.

Judy Hall

Zoo Journey
Sung to: "Frere Jacques"

I'm a lion, I'm a lion,
Hear me roar, hear me roar.
Roar, roar, roar,
Roar, roar, roar.
I am king, I am king.

I'm an elephant, I'm an elephant,
Hear me trumpet, hear me trumpet.
Trump, trump, trump,
Trump, trump, trump.
I am big, I am big.

I'm a tiger, I'm a tiger,
Hear me growl, hear me growl.
Growl, growl, growl,
Growl, growl, growl.
I am fierce, I am fierce.

Joelene Holley-Thomas

The Animals in the Zoo
Sung to: "The Farmer in the Dell"

The animals in the zoo,
Are smiling out at you.
They're glad that you could come
    today,
They hope that you can stay.

The seal is in the pool,
The seal is in the pool.
He knows how to keep so cool,
The seal is in the pool.

The turtle has a shell,
The turtle has a shell.
In her shell she hides so well,
The turtle has a shell.

The monkey is such fun,
The monkey is such fun.
He eats bananas in the sun,
The monkey is such fun.

The camel has a hump,
The camel has a hump.
When you ride her, you go bump,
The camel has a hump.

Barbara B. Fleisher

They All Live at the Zoo
Sung to: "Oh, Susanna"

Oh, the animals are many,
Now come on we'll name a few.
There're bears and deer and elephants,
They all live at the zoo.
Birds and turtles, zebras and kangaroos,
They are just a few of the animals
That you'll find at the zoo.

Judy Hall

Hear the Animals
Sung to: "She'll Be Coming Round the Mountain"

You will hear the lions roaring at the zoo,
You will hear the lions roaring at the zoo.
You will hear the lions roaring,
You will hear the lions roaring,
You will hear the lions roaring at the zoo.

Additional verses: "You will hear the snakes
hissing at the zoo; You will hear the bears
growling at the zoo."

Betty Silkunas

To the Zoo We'll Go
Sung to: "A-Hunting We Will Go"

To the zoo we'll go,
To the zoo we'll go.
Animals are everywhere,
To the zoo we'll go.

Lions all around,
Zebras can be found.
Monkeys swinging from the trees,
And making quite a sound.

Judy Hall

Take Me Out to the Zoo
Sung to: "Take Me Out to the Ball Game"

Take me out for some good fun,
Take me out to the zoo.
Let me visit the tall giraffe,
I want to hear the hyenas laugh.
Now I love to visit the zoo,
I could stay there all day,
And watch birds, seals, rhinos and
   hippos
As they play.

Cindy Dingwall

Through the Zoo
Sung to: "London Bridge"

Through the zoo I took a walk,
Took a walk, took a walk.
Through the zoo I took a walk,
And saw some animals.

A big gray elephant waved his trunk,
Waved his trunk, waved his trunk.
A big gray elephant waved his trunk,
At the zoo today.

A big old lion roared real loud,
Roared real loud, roared real loud.
A big old lion roared real loud,
At the zoo today.

A hippo wallowed in the water,
In the water, in the water.
A hippo wallowed in the water,
At the zoo today.

Cindy Dingwall

Here We Go to the Zoo
Sung to: "The Mulberry Bush"

Here we go to the zoo today,
Zoo today, zoo today.
Here we go to the zoo today,
To see the animals.

First the lion roars like this,
Roars like this, roars like this.
First the lion roars like this,
He's loud as he can be.

Then the elephant raises her trunk,
Raises her trunk, raises her trunk.
Then the elephant raises her trunk,
To wave to you and me.

The zebra's stripes are quite a sight,
Quite a sight, quite a sight.
The zebra's stripes are quite a sight,
Black and white, you see.

Judy Hall

The Blind Men and the Elephant

Tell the children this story from India about six blind men and an elephant. Display a picture of an elephant or a stuffed toy elephant to help the children visualize the story.

Six blind men went out one day to discover what an elephant was like. The first man touched the elephant's side and said, "An elephant is smooth like a wall." The second man touched the elephant's trunk and said, "An elephant is round like a snake." The third man touched the tusk of the elephant and said, "An elephant is sharp like a spear." The fourth man touched the elephant's leg and said, "An elephant is tall like a tree." The fifth man touched the ear of the elephant and said, "An elephant is wide like a fan." The sixth man touched the elephant's tail and said, "An elephant is thin like a rope." Finish the story anyway you wish. The moral of the story is that we must know all of the parts before we can find out the whole truth.

Retell the story but each time leave out different words for the children to fill in, such as what each man thought the elephant was like or the part of the elephant each man touched.

Zoo Riddles

Read the following riddles to the children. Let them guess which animals are described. Then help them make up their own riddles.

I have a long tail.
I live in trees.
I like to eat bananas.
(Monkey.)

I am big.
I have big ears.
I have a long nose.
(Elephant.)

I am king of the jungle.
I have a golden mane.
I like to roar.
(Lion.)

I am white.
I live where it is cold.
I eat fish for my dinner.
(Polar bear.)

I am pink.
I live where it is hot.
I have long legs.
(Flamingo.)

I look like a horse.
I like to run and play.
I have black and white stripes.
(Zebra.)

I like to eat leaves.
I have long legs.
I have a very long neck.
(Giraffe.)

Zoo Animal Story Bag

Place plastic zoo animals or pictures of zoo animals in a bag. Begin a story about going to the zoo. Stop every so often and let a child reach in the bag, pull out a zoo animal and name it. Incorporate the animal into your story. Continue until all the animals have been used.

Alligator Puppet Fun

Cut the lids off two egg cartons. Cut jagged teeth around three edges of each lid, leaving one short edge uncut. Put the lids together, with the teeth facing inward, and tape the uncut ends together. Cut two 1- by 6-inch strips out of construction paper and tape one near the back of the top lid and the other near the back of the bottom lid to make handles. Glue two cotton balls on the top lid and attach a plastic moving eye to each one. Let the children take turns using the alligator puppet while you recite the poem below.

Alligator, alligator, long and green.
Alligator, alligator, teeth so mean.
Snapping at a fly,
Snapping at a bee,
Snapping at a frog,
But you can't catch me!

Jean Warren

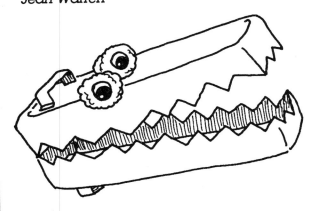

Elephant Puppet

Cut a small circle out of the side of a paper cup to make a nose hole. Add eyes and a mouth with felt-tip markers. Glue pieces of gray felt or paper cut in the shape of elephants' ears to the sides of the cup. Stick a finger into the cup and out the hole to make an elephant's trunk. Let the children take turns using the elephant puppet while you recite the following poem.

Elephant, elephant in the zoo,
I wish I had a trunk like you.
I'd swing it high,
I'd swing it low.
I'd swing it everywhere I go!

Jean Warren

Language Puppets

Let the children play with a variety of zoo animal puppets. Encourage them to make their puppets talk. Ask the children such questions as "What do you like to eat? What makes you happy? Who do you like to play with?" Let the children use the animal puppets while reciting favorite animal rhymes or singing favorite animal songs.

Zoo Stories

Using the patterns on the following pages as guides, cut zoo animal shapes out of pieces of felt. Place the shapes on a flannelboard and encourage the children to make up stories about them. Or use the zoo animal shapes to illustrate children's stories about the zoo.

Children's Books About the Zoo

The Adventures of Albert the Running Bear, Barbara Isenberg (Houghton Mifflin).
Color Zoo, Lois Ehlert (Harper).
I'm in the Zoo, Too!, Brent Ashabranner (Dutton).
Sam Who Never Forgets, Eve Rice (Viking).
Where's Wallace?, Hilary Knight (Harper).
Zoo, Gail Gibbons (Harper).

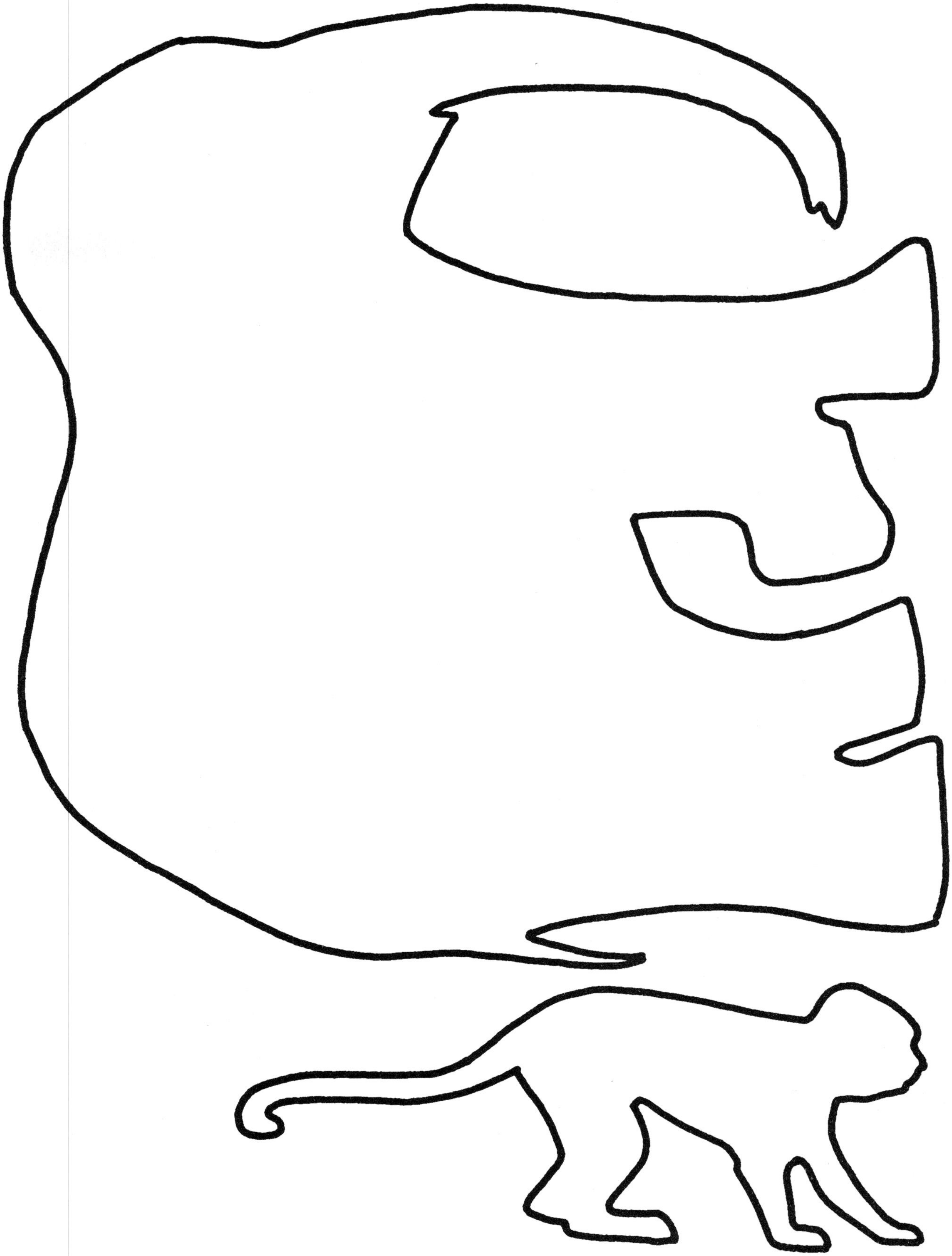

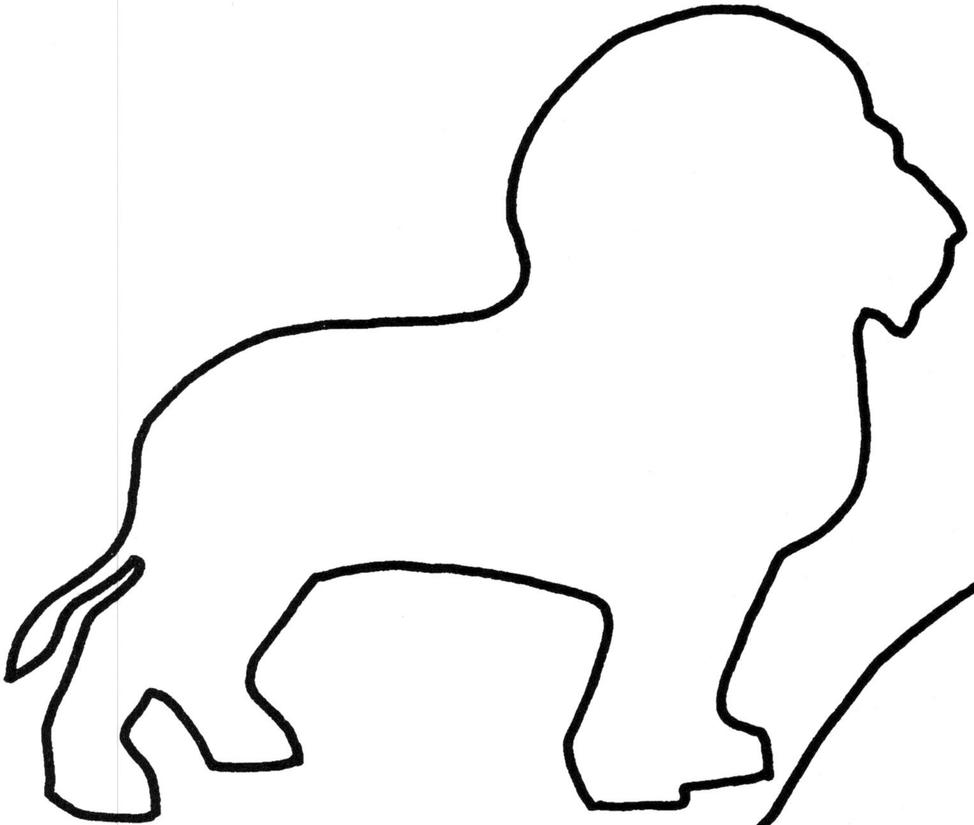

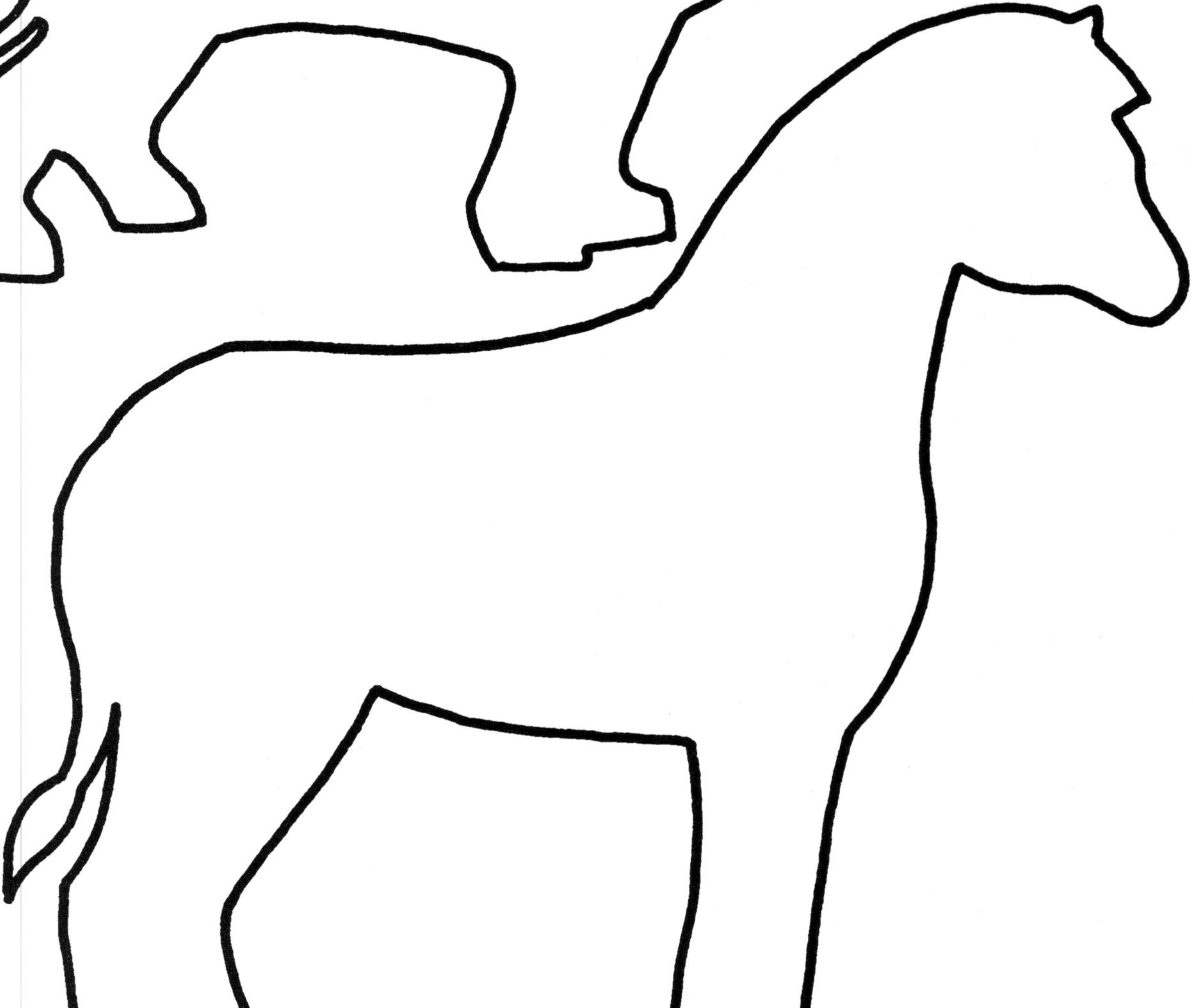

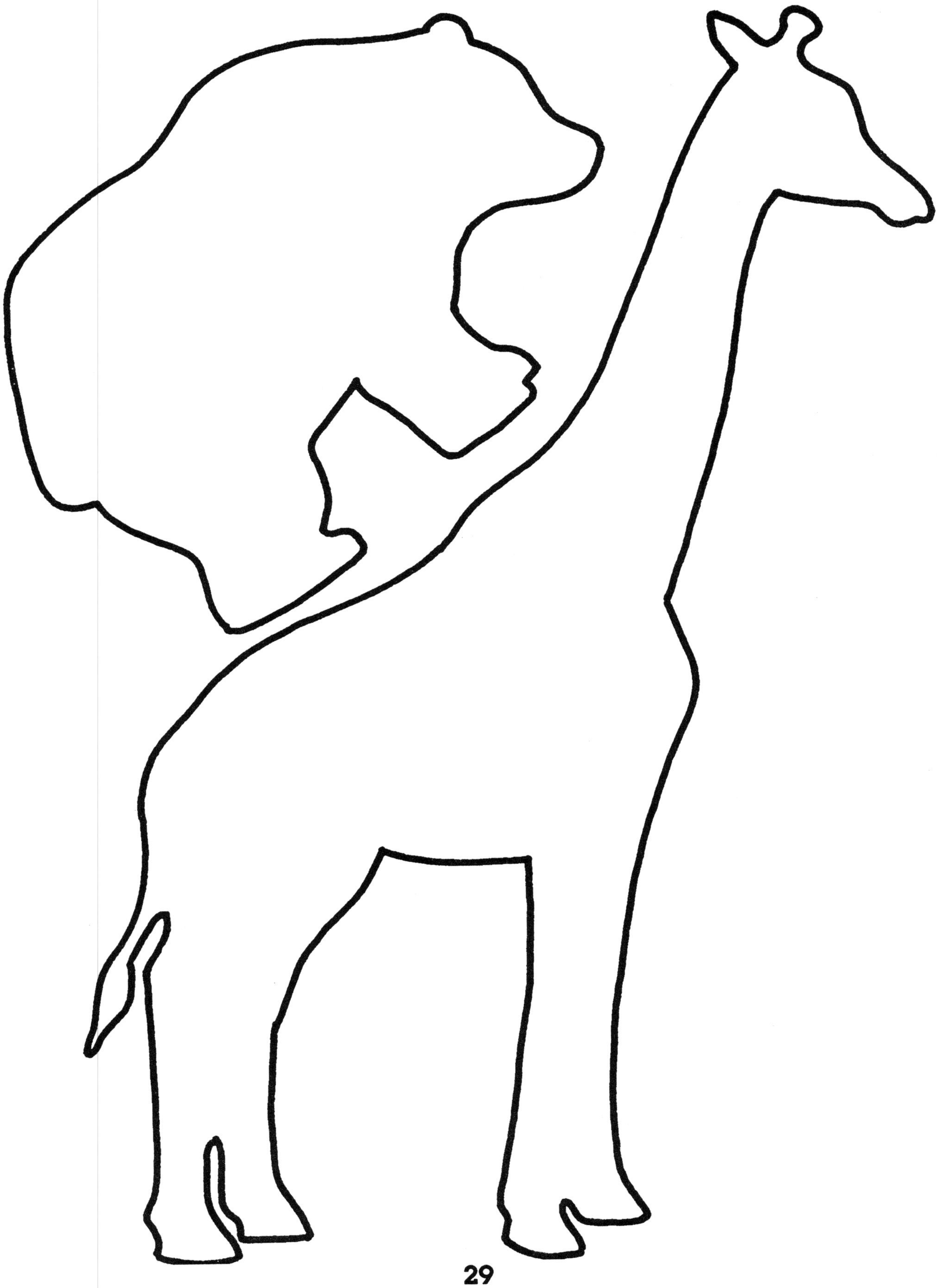

Who's Hiding in the Zoo?

Place a piece of cardboard inside a large envelope. Use a utility knife to cut four large flaps in front of the envelope. Remove the cardboard and slide a picture of a zoo animal into the envelope. Raise one of the flaps and let the children guess what animal is shown in the picture. Continue raising different flaps until someone guesses the animal.

Feelie Zoo

Place plastic zoo animals, one at a time, in a feelie box. Let the children take turns putting their hands in the box and trying to guess what the animal is by feeling its shape.

Variation: Instead of using a feelie box, let the children take turns holding their hands behind their backs. Place small plastic animals in their hands. Then let the children guess what animals they are holding.

Texture Game

Choose three zoo animals with different textured hides such as an alligator, a bear and a zebra. Glue pictures of them on small index cards. Glue corresponding pieces of hide made out of fake fur, vinyl or leather on other index cards. Set out the animal hide cards and let the children select the animal cards and place them below the appropriate animal hide cards.

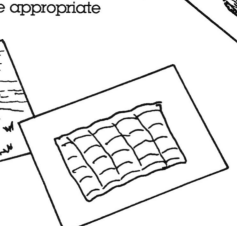

Zoo Environments

Let the children create environments for zoo animals in a dishpan filled with sand or at a sand table. Provide small leaves, ferns, twigs and branches for the children to use to create their zoo settings. Give the children plastic zoo animals to play with in their zoo environments.

Zoo Flannelboard Fun

Using the animal patterns on pages 25 to 29 as guides, cut zoo animal shapes out of felt. Cut out five each of the six different animals. Use the animal shapes in the following games.

Sorting — Mix up the animal shapes and let the children sort them into sets.

Matching — Place several zoo animals in a parade across the top of a flannelboard. Have the children place matching animals in a line below them.

Counting — Use the animal shapes while singing animal counting songs or reciting counting rhymes.

Number Match-Ups

Number six large index cards from 1 to 6, writing the numerals on the left hand sides of the cards. On the right hand sides of the cards place a corresponding number of zoo animal stickers. Cover each card with clear self-stick paper for durability. Cut each card in half differently, creating six mini-puzzles. Mix up the cards and let the children take turns matching the correct number of animal stickers with the numerals.

Zoo Alphabet Cards

Use the zoo alphabet cards on the following pages to make these or other learning games. Or photocopy a set for each child to make a zoo alphabet book.

Lotto — Divide a piece of posterboard into nine equal sections. Select nine of the alphabet cards and make two photocopies of each one. Glue one set of the cards to the posterboard, one card in each section. Cover the posterboard and the other set of cards with clear self-stick paper. Let the children match the individual cards to the ones glued on the posterboard.

Concentration — Photocopy and cut apart two sets of the alphabet cards. Cover the cards with clear self-stick paper, if desired. Have the children place them face down on a table. Let one child draw two cards. If the cards match, have the child keep both cards and draw again. If the cards do not match, have the child replace the cards and let another child draw two cards. Continue the game until all of the cards have been matched.

Aa

alligator

Bb

bear

Cc

camel

Dd

donkey

Ee

elephant

Ff

flamingo

Gg

giraffe

Hh

hippopotamus

Ii

iguana

Jj

jaguar

Kk

kangaroo

Ll

lion

Mm

monkey

Nn

nest

Oo

ostrich

Pp

penguin

Qq

quail

Rr

rhinoceros

Ss

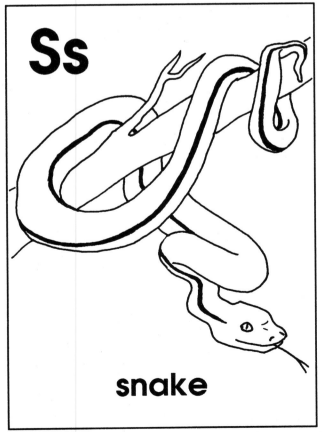

snake

Tt

tiger

Uu Vv

Ww

walrus

Xx Yy

Zz

zebra

Totline® Newsletter

Activities, songs and new ideas to use right now are waiting for you in every issue!

Each issue puts the fun into teaching with 32 pages of challenging and creative activities for young children. Included are open-ended art activities, learning games, music, language and science activities plus 8 reproducible pattern pages.

Published bi-monthly.

Sample issue - $2.00

Super Snack News

Nutritious snack ideas, related songs, rhymes and activities

- Teach young children health and nutrition through fun and creative activities.

- Use as a handout to involve parents in their children's education.

- Promote quality child care in the community with these handouts.

- Includes nutritious sugarless snacks, health tidbits, and developmentally appropriate activities.

- Includes CACFP information for most snacks.

With each subscription you are given the right to:

Make up to: **200 COPIES** per issue

Published monthly.

Sample issue - $2.00

Exploring Books

NEW!

Confused by the large number of new children's books published each year?

Need help in selecting just the right titles for your library or classroom needs?

Then you need *Exploring Books*, the children's book review for librarians and teachers of young children - each filled with over 50 reviews of new and theme related titles plus tips on using children's books to teach.

Published quarterly.

Sample issue - $2.00

Warren Publishing House, Inc. • P.O. Box 2250, Dept. Z • Everett, WA 98203

Totline Books

Piggyback® Songs

More Piggyback® Songs

Piggyback® Songs
    for Infants and Toddlers

Piggyback® Songs
    in Praise of God

Piggyback® Songs
    in Praise of Jesus

Holiday Piggyback® Songs

Animal Piggyback® Songs

Piggyback® Songs for School

1·2·3 Art

1·2·3 Games

1·2·3 Colors

1·2·3 Puppets

1·2·3 Murals

1·2·3 Books

1·2·3 Reading & Writing

1·2·3 Rhymes, Stories & Songs

Teeny-Tiny Folktales

Short-Short Stories

Mini-Mini Musicals

Small World Celebrations

Special Day Celebrations

Yankee Doodle
    Birthday Celebrations

Great Big Holiday Celebrations

"Cut & Tell"
    Scissor Stories for Fall

"Cut & Tell"
    Scissor Stories for Winter

"Cut & Tell"
    Scissor Stories for Spring

Alphabet Theme-A-Saurus®

Theme-A-Saurus®

Theme-A-Saurus® II

Toddler Theme-A-Saurus®

Alphabet & Number Rhymes

Color, Shape & Season Rhymes

Object Rhymes

Animal Rhymes

Our World

Our Selves

Animal Patterns

Everyday Patterns

Holiday Patterns

Nature Patterns

ABC Space

ABC Farm

ABC Zoo

ABC Circus

1001 Teaching Props

Super Snacks

Available at school supply stores and parent/teacher stores or write for our catalog.

Warren Publishing House, Inc. • P.O. Box 2250, Dept. B • Everett, WA 98203